Memorial Of Alexander Hamilton McGuffey

Jacob Dolson Cox

In the interest of creating a more extensive selection of rare historical book reprints, we have chosen to reproduce this title even though it may possibly have occasional imperfections such as missing and blurred pages, missing text, poor pictures, markings, dark backgrounds and other reproduction issues beyond our control. Because this work is culturally important, we have made it available as a part of our commitment to protecting, preserving and promoting the world's literature. Thank you for your understanding.

MEMORIAL

OF

Alexander Hamilton McGuffey

Adopted by the Trustees of Cincinnati College

CINCINNATI
THE ROBERT CLARKE COMPANY
1896

MEMORIAL

OF

Alexander Hamilton McGuffey.

This memorial was prepared by General Jacob D. Cox, was referred to a committee consisting of Hon. Jacob D. Cox, Rt. Revd. Boyd Vincent, D.D. Mr. Obed J. Wilson, Mr. John A. Gano, and Col. Sidney D. Maxwell. It was reported by them, and was unanimously adopted as the voice of the Board of Trustees. Thereupon it was ordered that the same be printed for the use of the Board.

Done at the meeting of June 6, 1896.

Wm. Howard Neff,
President.

Alexander Hamilton McGuffey.

In the death of ALEXANDER HAMILTON MCGUFFEY, Cincinnati has lost one of its oldest and most respected citizens. Few indeed are the survivors whose lives reach back to the pioneer period, when Ohio was almost a continuous forest, and the farms of its settlers were sparsely scattered openings in the nearly unbroken woods. What are now its great cities were then mere villages, and its thriving county seats were only hamlets at the cross-roads.

He was born on the 13th of August, 1816, on the Western Reserve, close to the border of Pennsylvania, but all his mature life was spent in Cincinnati, and he died at his home on Mt. Auburn on the 3d of June, 1896, when he was within a few weeks of completing his eightieth year. He was of Scotch parentage, and the family was an intellectual one. His elder brother, the Rev. William H. McGuffey, was in 1825 the President of the Miami University at Oxford, beginning the career of an eminent educator, which culminated in his professorship of philosophy in the University of Virginia many years afterward.

President McGuffey took charge of the education of his brother, Alexander, when the latter was only nine years of age, but already a studious youth. Such indeed was his talent and strong scholarly bent that he completed his college course and graduated at the very early age of sixteen. To so brilliant a collegian it was a matter of course that he should be invited to teach, and he soon became professor of ancient languages in Woodward College, from that time making Cincinnati his home. He was admitted to the bar as soon as he reached his majority, and for nearly sixty years he was an honored member of the legal profession. His tastes led him to seek the quieter walks of business, and the greater part of his life was spent in chamber practice as a counsellor, especially in the management of trusts and the settlement of estates. He was methodical and extremely accurate, conducting business with systematic thoroughness. In arguments he was logical and keen rather than oratorical, and took pleasure in the analysis of strictly legal questions of property rights rather than in appeals to a jury.

His scholarly training and his love of literature found employments collateral to his professional work, especially in his first year at the bar. He was the active collaborator with President McGuffey in the compilation of McGuffey's Readers, the most popular series of school books published west of the Allegheny Mountains.* It is understood that the Fifth Reader in the series, so well known for its exquisite selections from a very broad field in English literature, was wholly his work, as was the "Speller," which completed the series. It alone sufficiently shows his early and wide acquaintance with the masterpieces of our language, and his solid judgment in drawing from the "well of English undefiled." His fondness for the classics in our own and in the ancient tongues lasted through his

---

* It is due to the memory of Mr. Winthrop B. Smith, the very enterprising publisher of that early time, to say that the origination of the plan for the series of Readers was his.

life and was a perennial source of pleasure to him and to his friends. He had, too, the gift of a racy humor and a skill with the pencil which, in the way of illustration and caricature, often charmed the circle of his intimates.

Yet most people knew him as he appeared to casual acquaintances—a reticent, earnest man, of strong will and tenacity of purpose, self-reliant and self-contained, not feeling, apparently, the need of taking others into his confidence, or of explaining the motives of his conduct, so sure was he of the high conscientiousness which ruled his life. There was much of the old Scotch Covenanter in his downright dealing and his sharply-defined ideas of duty and of right, but there was also a refinement of feeling, an unostentatious sympathy and a charitable judgment of men, which was none the less real, though he shrank from its display. This inner character, as the complement of his outward traits, was well typified and illustrated in his religious life. Brought up a Presbyterian, his early church membership was with the Second Church, when Lyman Beecher was its pastor, but later in life he united with the Protestant Episcopal Church. One side of his nature responded to the stern discipline of Calvin, but on the other he was drawn to the historic dignity and richness of the English liturgy.

In the Church in which he spent most of his life, he was not sparing of his labor. From youth to age he was active in all the duties which fall to a layman. In his own parish he was vestryman or warden. In the diocese he was for many years a member of the Standing Committee, the regular advisers of the bishop in business matters. It was seldom that he was absent from diocesan or general conventions of the Church, and in these he was recognized as an authority in canon law. During the whole period of his manhood such duties made up no inconsiderable part of his life work, and he gave his time and labor freely and ungrudgingly.

His connection with the Corporation of the Cincinnati College was that by which he was most generally known to the public. Nowhere was his work more disinterested or more valuable. A double duty seemed to call him—his strong zeal in higher education, and a filial interest in the work of his distinguished father-in-law, Dr. Daniel Drake, one of the ornaments of the intellectual life of early Cincinnati. From the grant of the college charter in 1819, Dr. Drake had been its mainstay. It was hoped that a commodious college building would be a basis for a college, drawing to its able faculty students enough, at reasonable rates of tuition, to support its teachers. In those early days academies were supported altogether in that way, and it was not unreasonable to suppose that the demand for a higher grade in education would support a collegiate institution on the modest scale which marked a time when the apparatus of instruction was primitive and simple. For a time it succeeded, but it was a transition period, and both the Cincinnati College and Woodward College soon found that without a large fixed income the modern scheme of college education can not be supported.

The extension of public support to high schools led the way to the idea of free education in the highest academic courses, and both the colleges of Cincinnati had to yield to the logic of events. Their record had been an honorable one, and their professors had been men of eminent learning and ability, who were soon called to chairs in richer institutions; but the idea of self-supporting colleges had to be abandoned. Woodward was transformed into the more useful work of a model high school, and the Cincinnati College, after tentative efforts of various kinds, became a college of law by its absorption of the Cincinnati Law School. It is interesting to note also that the considerable endowment founded by Charles McMicken for an orphan asylum and school for boys and girls could not compete with the public system of free education in the lower grades, and the law of natural development wisely fostered by the McMicken trustees led to a co-operation with the public in collegiate work. Thus, out of three institutions in which Cincinnatians ought to take pride, there have grown three, neither of which is in the form attempted by the founders, but all are the more useful because they have been molded by the law of natural selection, accepted and wisely furthered by the several Boards of Trustees.

In the case of the Cincinnati College, Mr. McGuffey had a leading part in the transition I have sketched. Fire had twice destroyed College Building, and the last re-building had only been accomplished by putting the property in the hands of mortgage trustees to pay off the debt from the rents and profits. This implied that every available part of the building should be rented and made profitable in money before the resumption of profitable education could be dreamed of. A weary series of years passed by before this was accomplished, but it ended at last and the property was handed back to its College Trustees. They had made Mr. McGuffey their secretary and treasurer in 1845, and from that day to the day of his death he nursed its business interests with so devoted a zeal that cynical people, who have a way of echoing Satan's question, "Does Job serve God for naught?" were ready to believe that he had made the property his own. Conscious of his disinterested devotion to a good cause, he did not break over his habitual silence in regard to himself, and bore for years a burden of misjudgment that would have greatly galled a less self-poised man.

His vindication came in the quo warranto proceedings, in which the college charter was sustained, a couple of years ago, when the records of the board were put in evidence, and it was seen that he had not a copper of profit in all that he had done for the college, and had only received the modest fees for the collection and disbursements of rents which are given to the humblest agent or collector.

But what had he done? He had found that in the long period of discouragement many of the statutory share-holders, who are the constituency behind educational trustees, had been lost sight of. Some had died and left no known heirs. Some had moved away from the city and dropped from memory. Some feared possible responsibility, and would not act. Some were simply indifferent and neglectful. Mr. McGuffey went patiently to work to correct this. He stimulated the interest of those who could be stirred to a sense of duty. He induced the indifferent to assign their share to others who would be faithful to a charitable trust. He bought some shares with his own money and assigned them without price to leading citizens who would enter heartily into the work of preserving and applying to educational purposes the college property and its income. He induced leading citizens of highest character to serve on the board, so that the list of former trustees is one of which any institution might well be proud. He thus brought together in revived and wholesome activity a harmonious constituency pledged to perpetuate a valuable charitable foundation, in accordance with the provisions of its charter.

Under his leadership, varied educational interests were assisted. For a considerable term of years the art school had free quarters in the building, and only left when an endowment of its own enabled it voluntarily to resign its rooms in the college. Courses of scientific and other lectures were given in College Hall as long as the popular lecture system remained in vogue. In every feasible way the college showed hospitality to sound educational efforts.

Of course, all this was done by the board of trustees, but it is only honest to say that in it all Mr. McGuffey was the prompter and leader, always alert to see what could be done and to stimulate the members of the corporation to do it. It is but just to him to say that his was a rare and conspicuous example of an able man devoting the best energies of a lifetime to a noble purpose, which he made so completely his own that time, labor, and cost were forgotten—as much as if he were nourishing his child. He thus earned his title of Father of the Cincinnati College.

His sympathy was extended to every educational work. He served for many years as president of the board of trustees of the Miami Medical College, and for some time as one of the board of directors of the University of Cincinnati.

In this brief memorial of our departed friend, it remains only to complete the record of his personal and family life. Mr. McGuffey was twice married. In 1839 he married Miss Elizabeth M. Drake, the daughter of Dr. Daniel Drake, by whom he had a large family of sons and daughters. After her death, he married Miss Caroline V. Rich, daughter of the late Samuel H. Rich, of Boston. Mrs. McGuffey, with her two daughters and a son, survive him. There was much that was patriarchal in his life during his declining years. His children and his children's children followed him with love and reverence, and he saw the good fruit of his own life and principles in their useful lives and honored stations. He retained remarkable physical activity nearly to the end. No acute disease prostrated him, but at the close of the winter his bodily powers gradually failed, and without much pain he slowly and peacefully faded away.

Printed by Libri Plureos GmbH in Hamburg, Germany